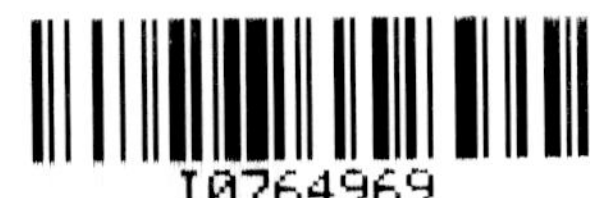

ARCTIC ANIMALS COLORING BOOK

RUBY SLIPPERS PUBLISHING

This Coloring Book Belongs To:

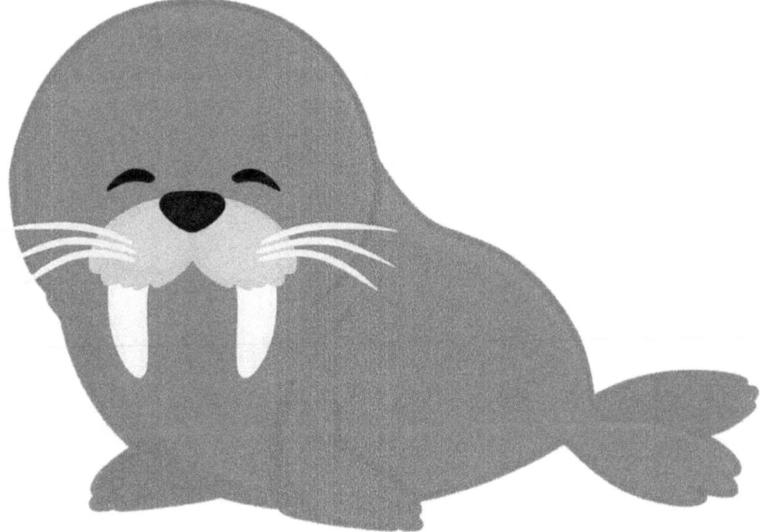

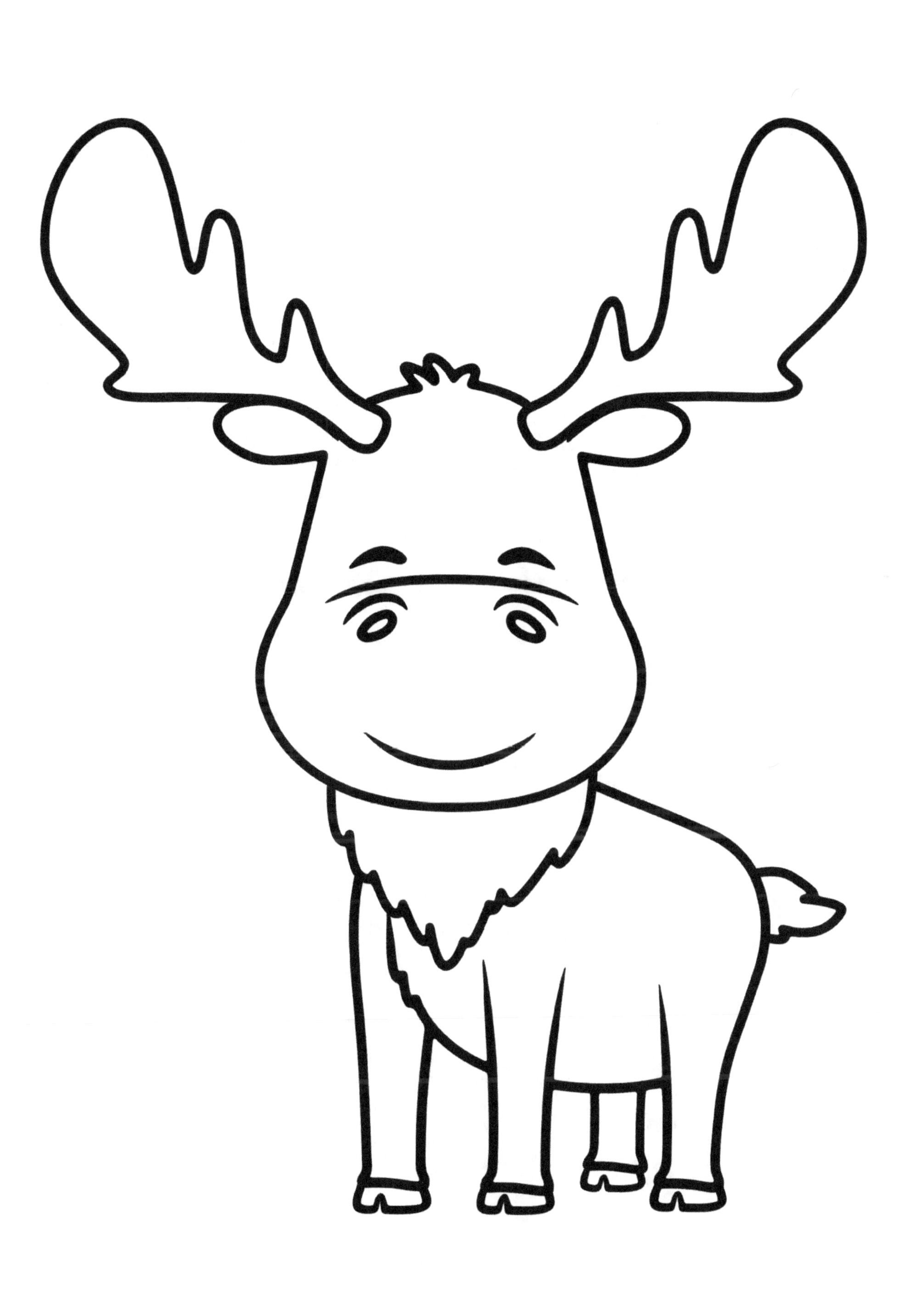

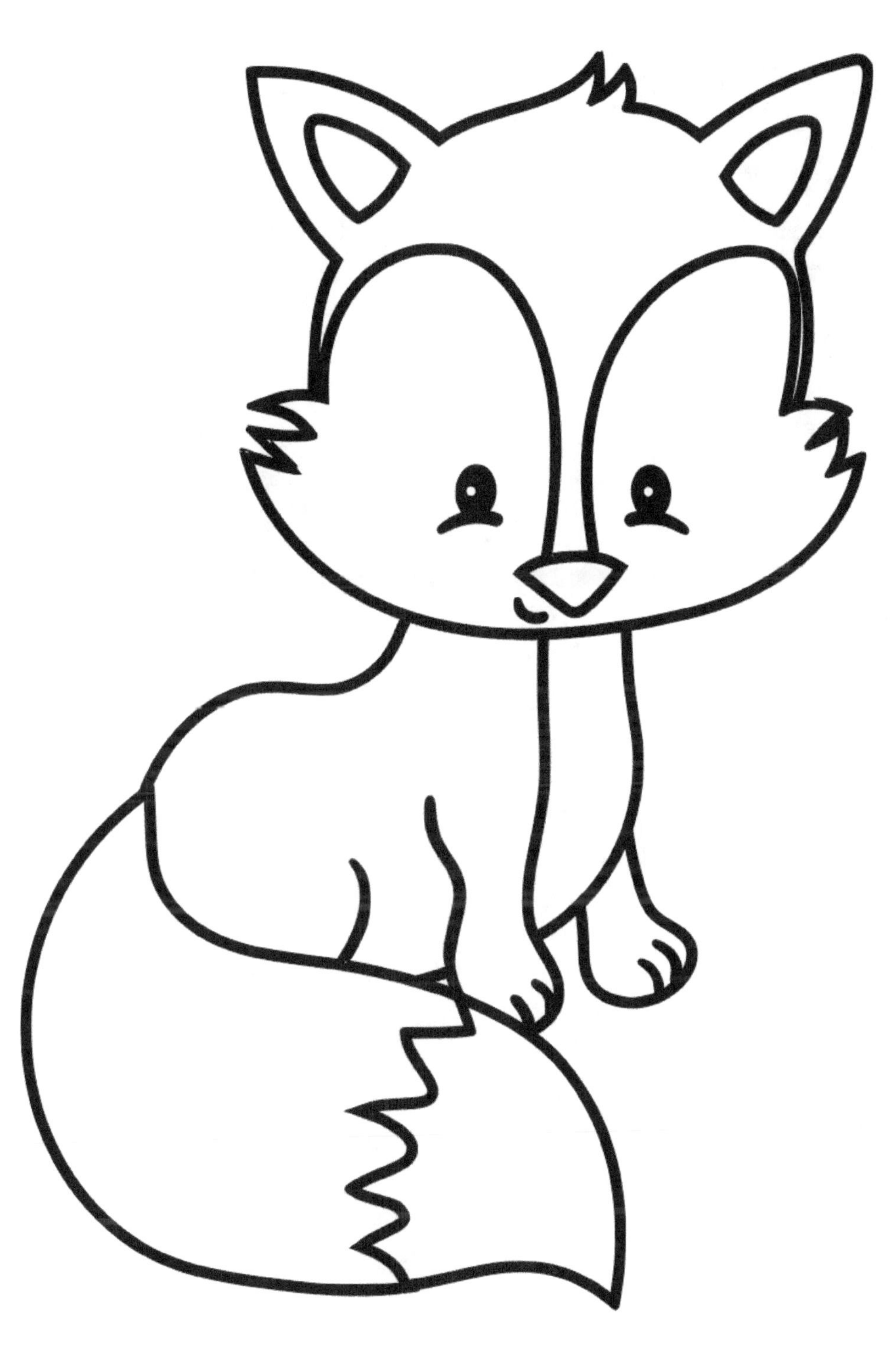

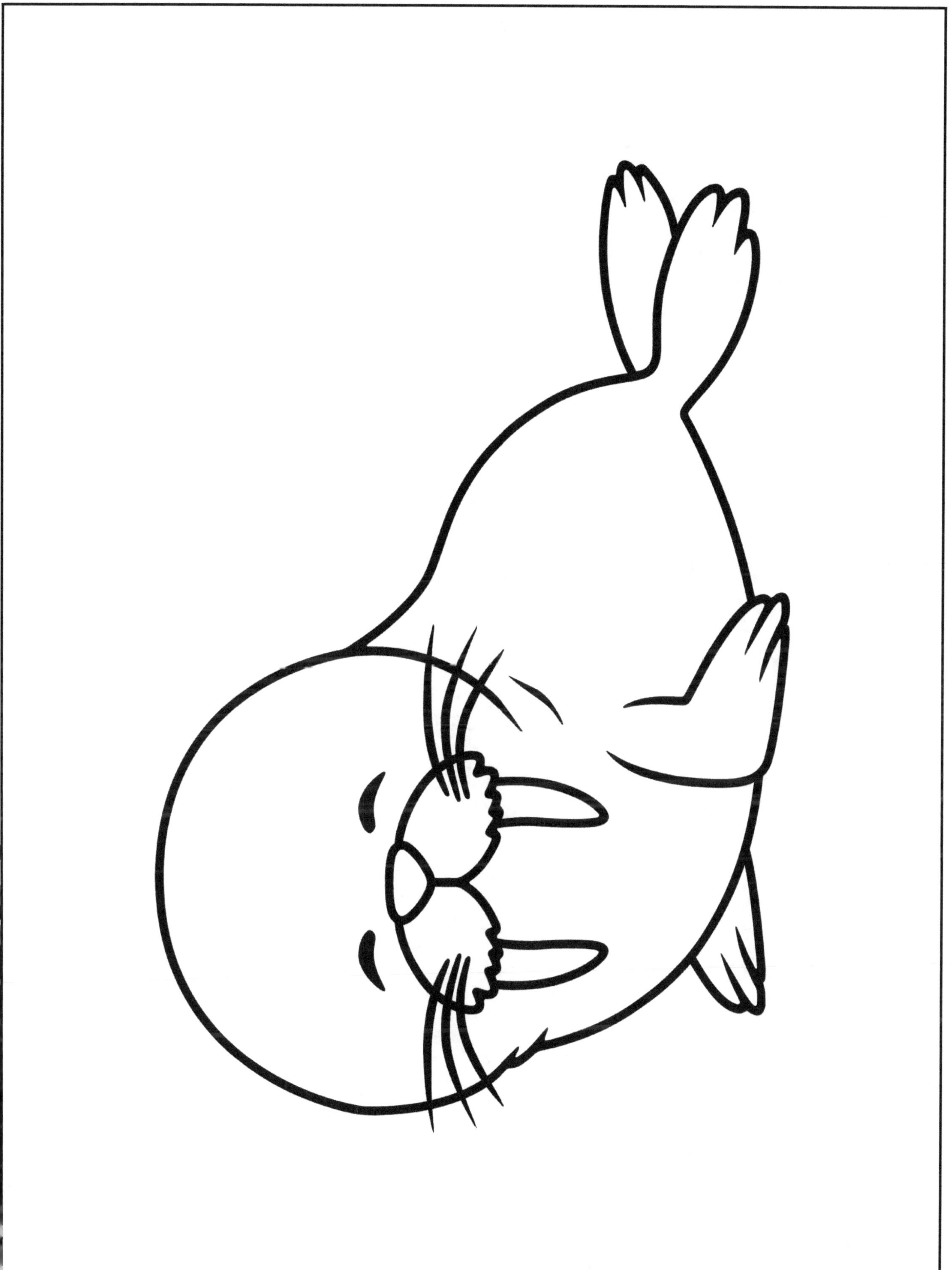

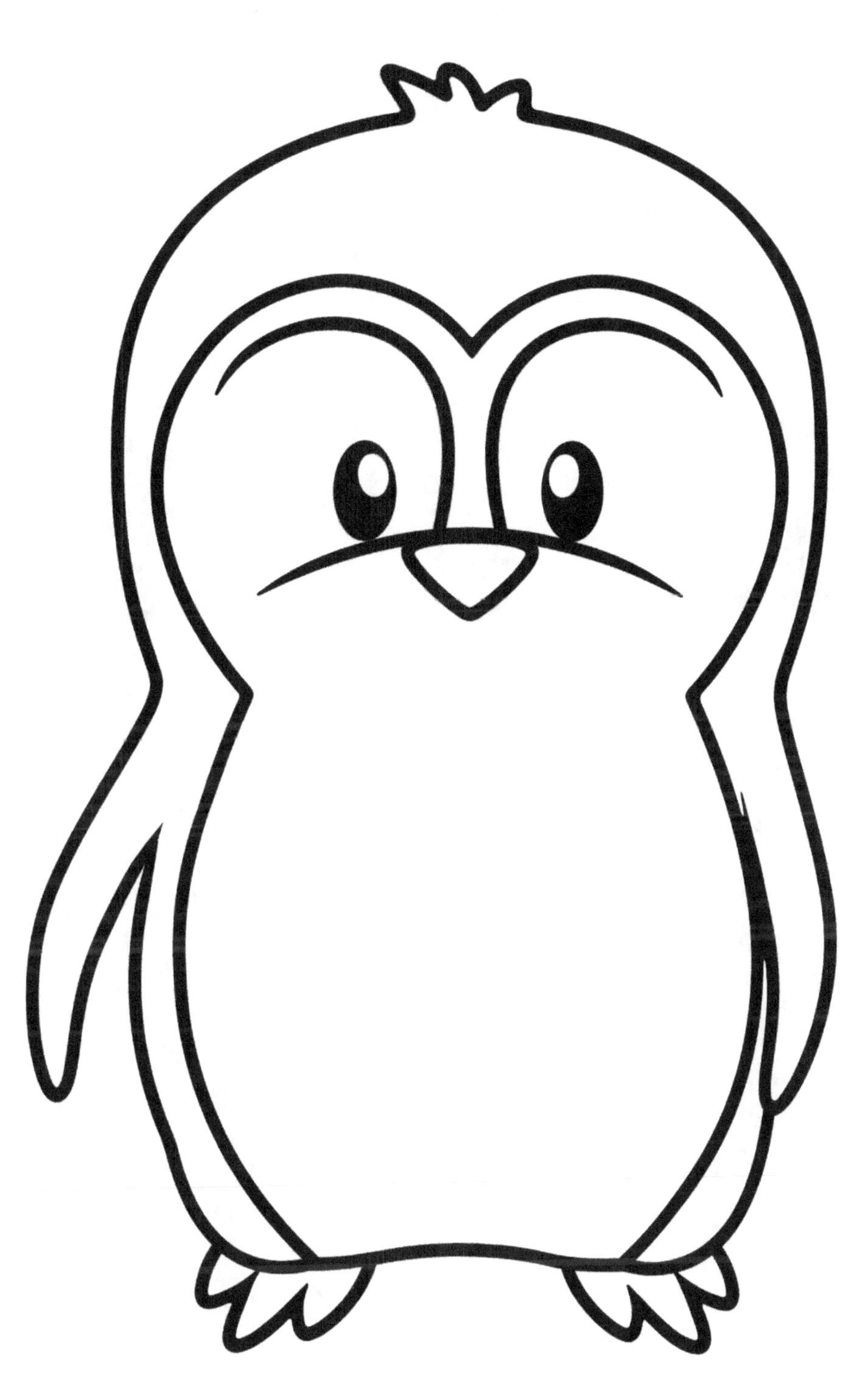

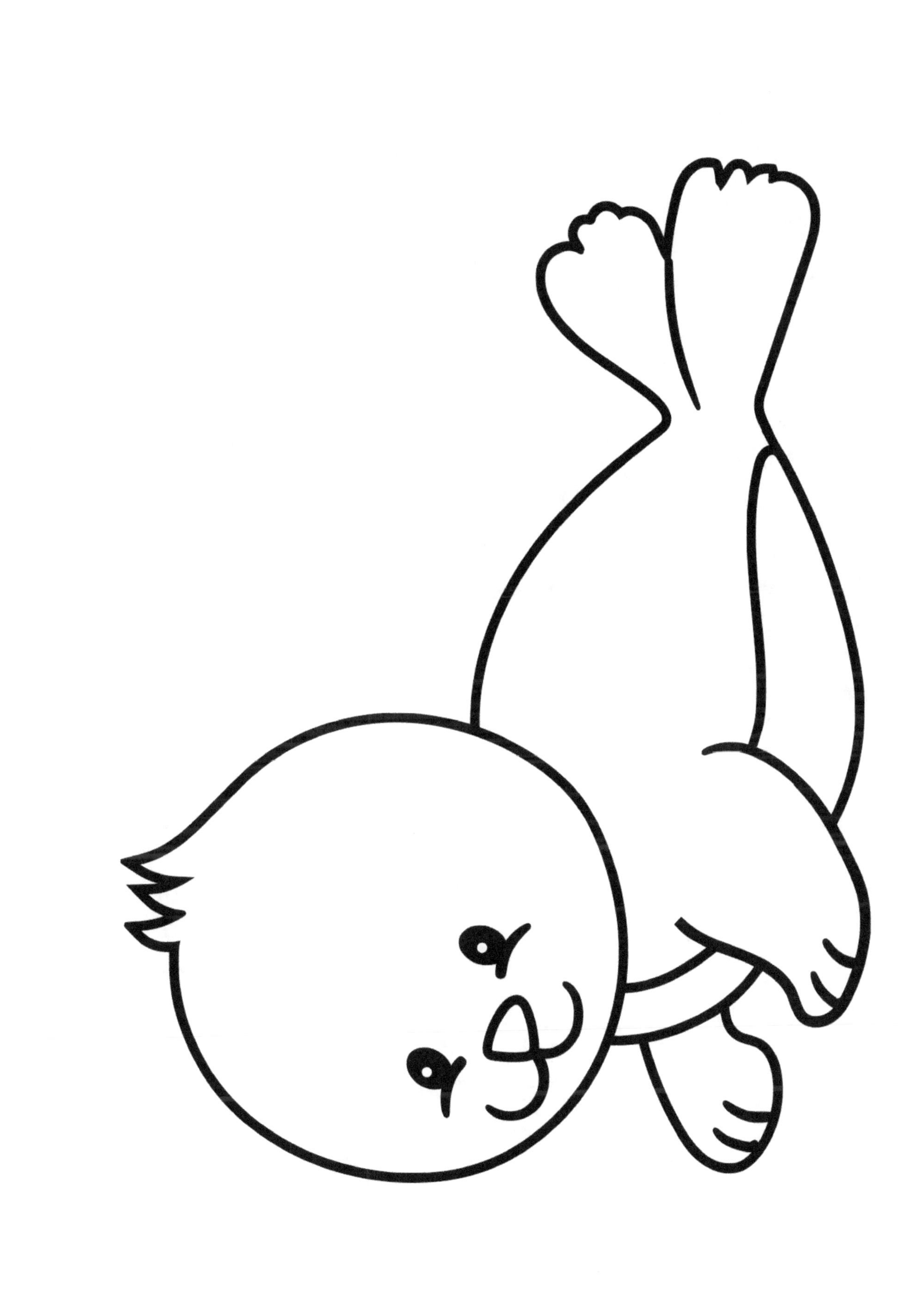

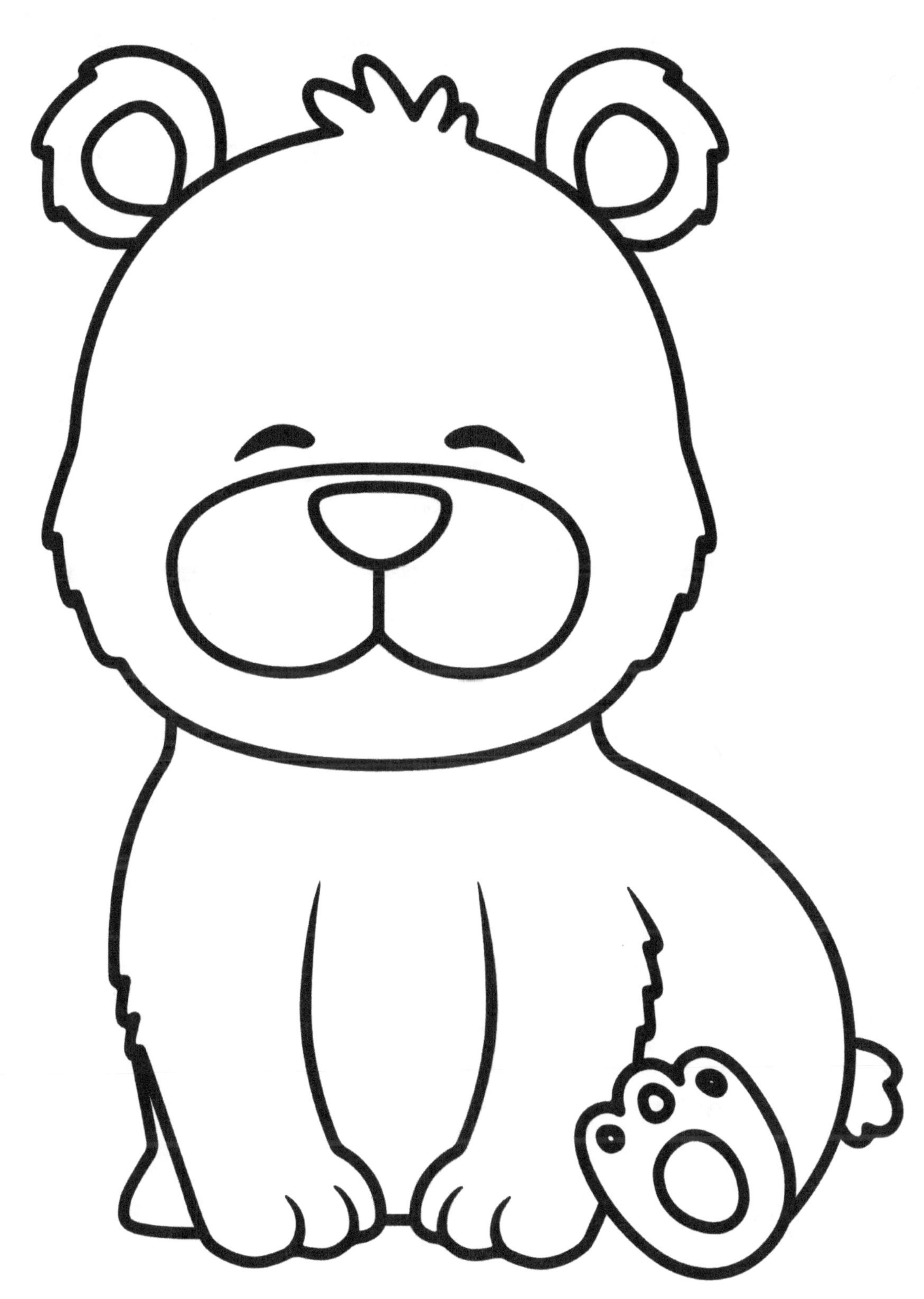

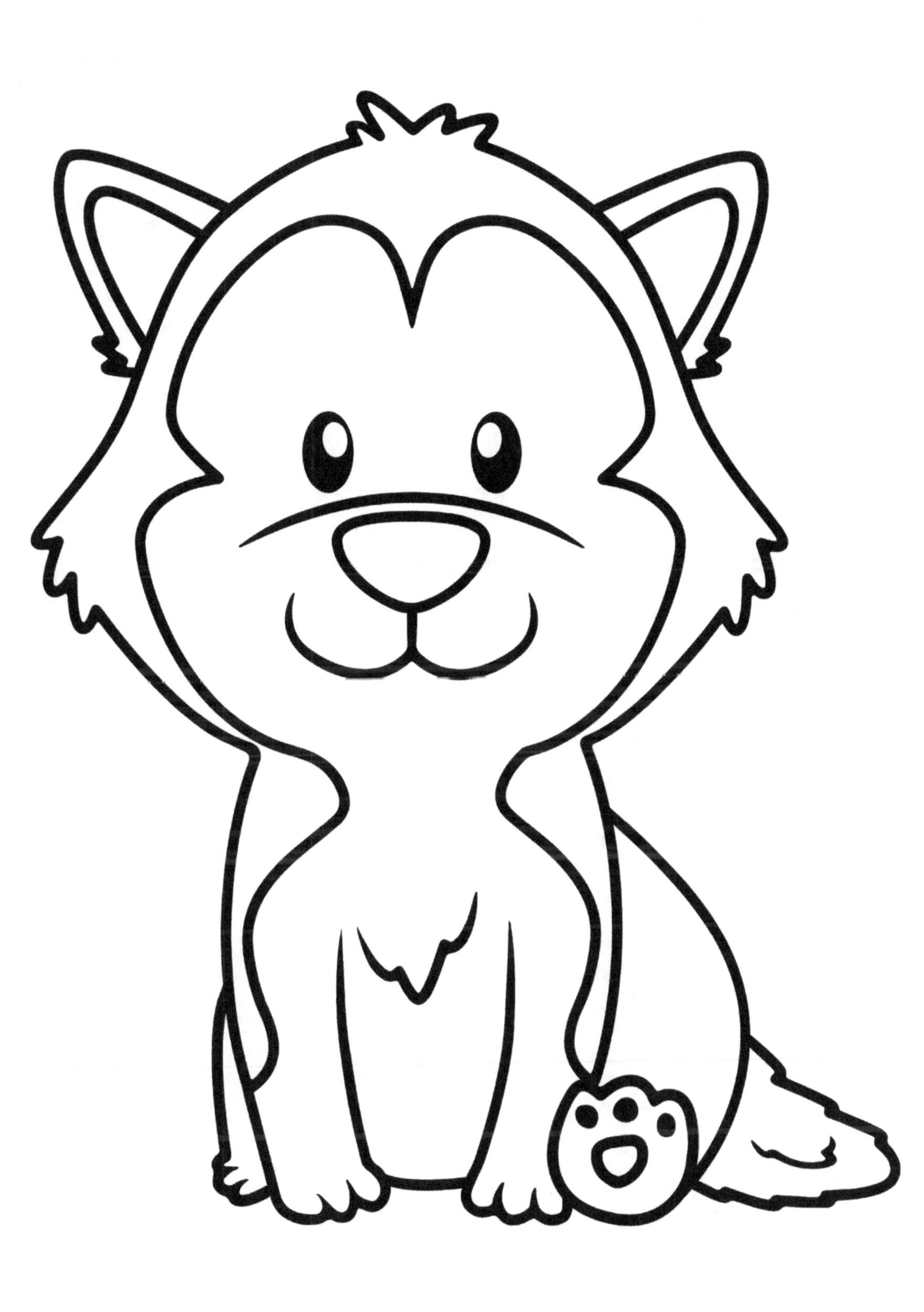

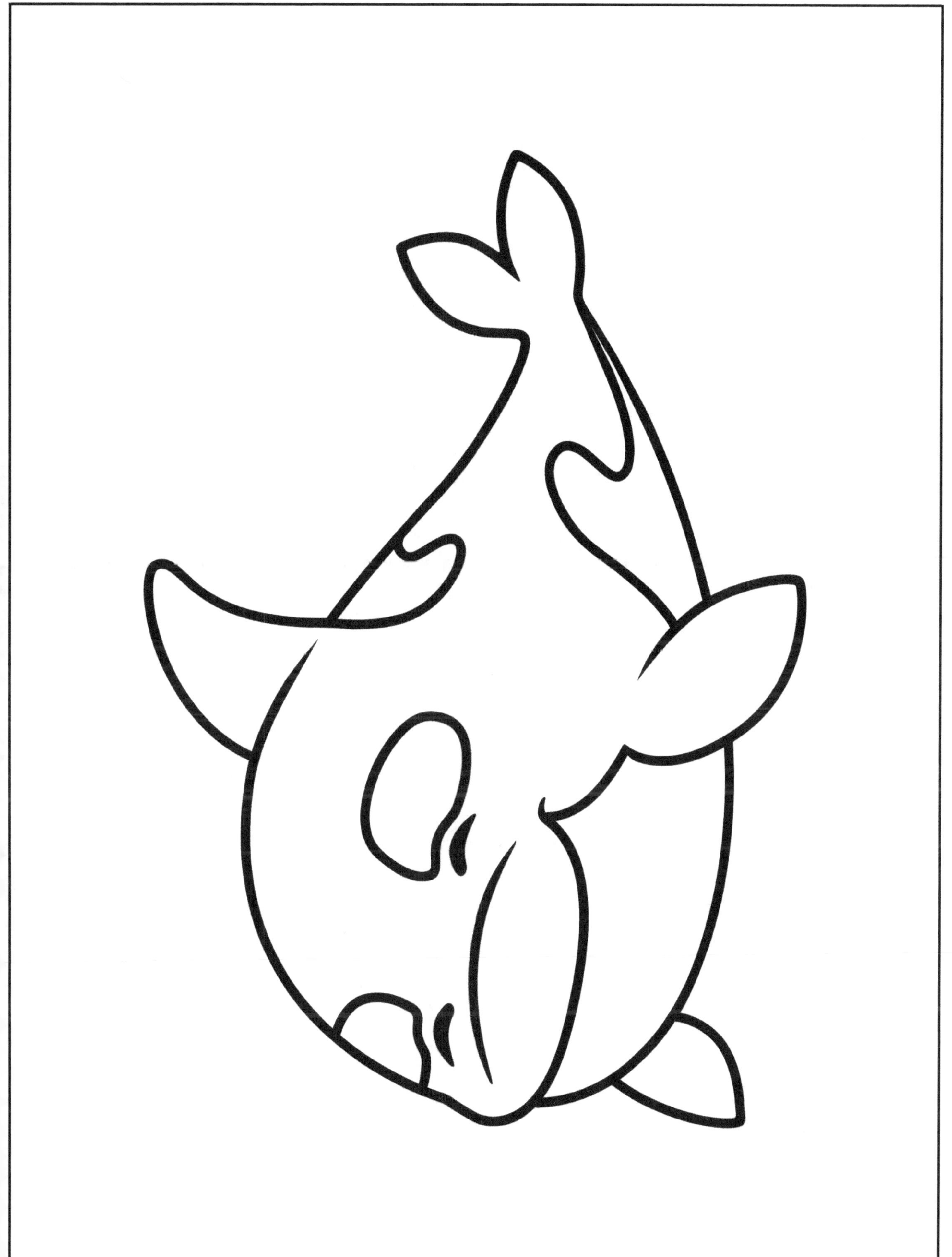

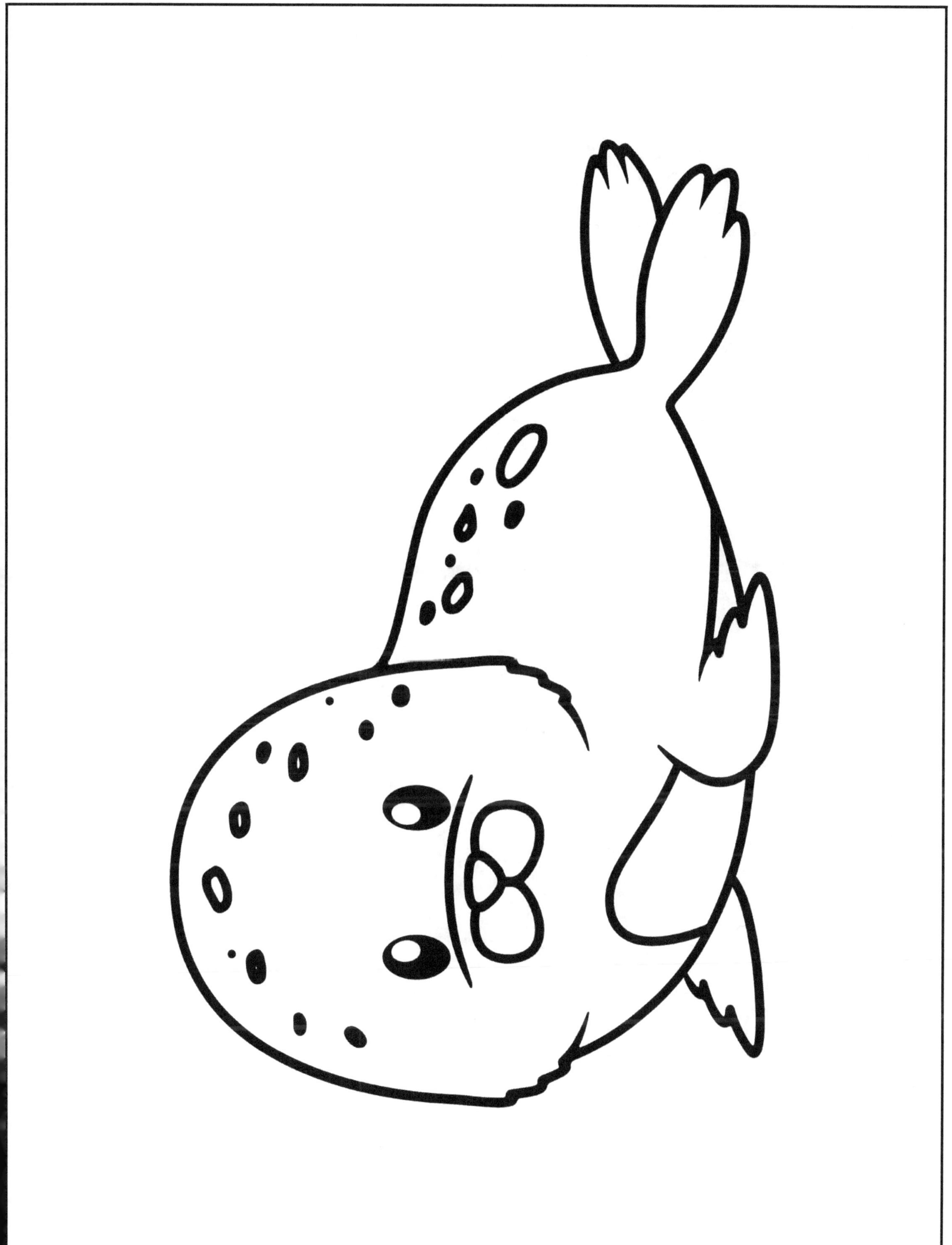

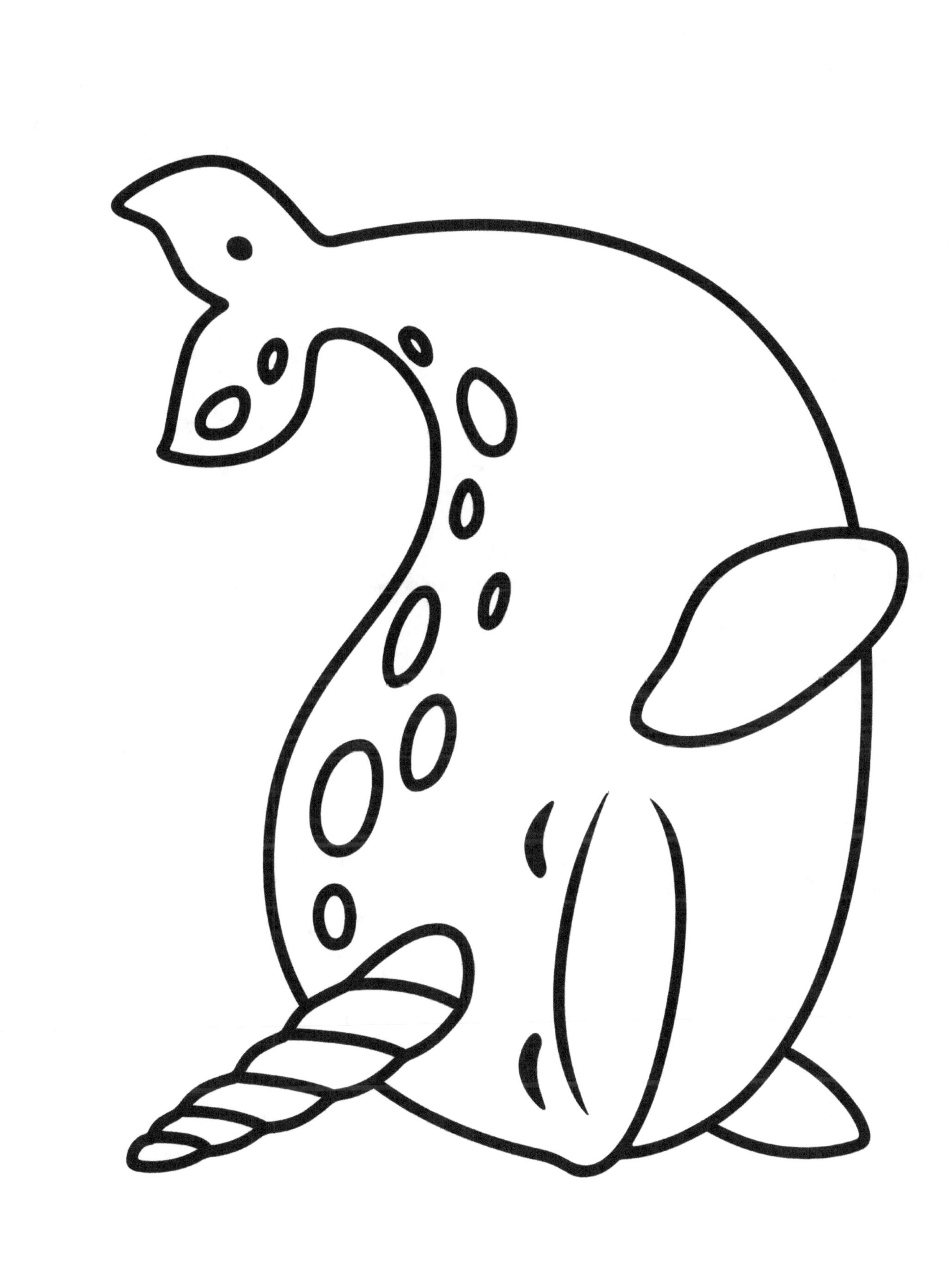

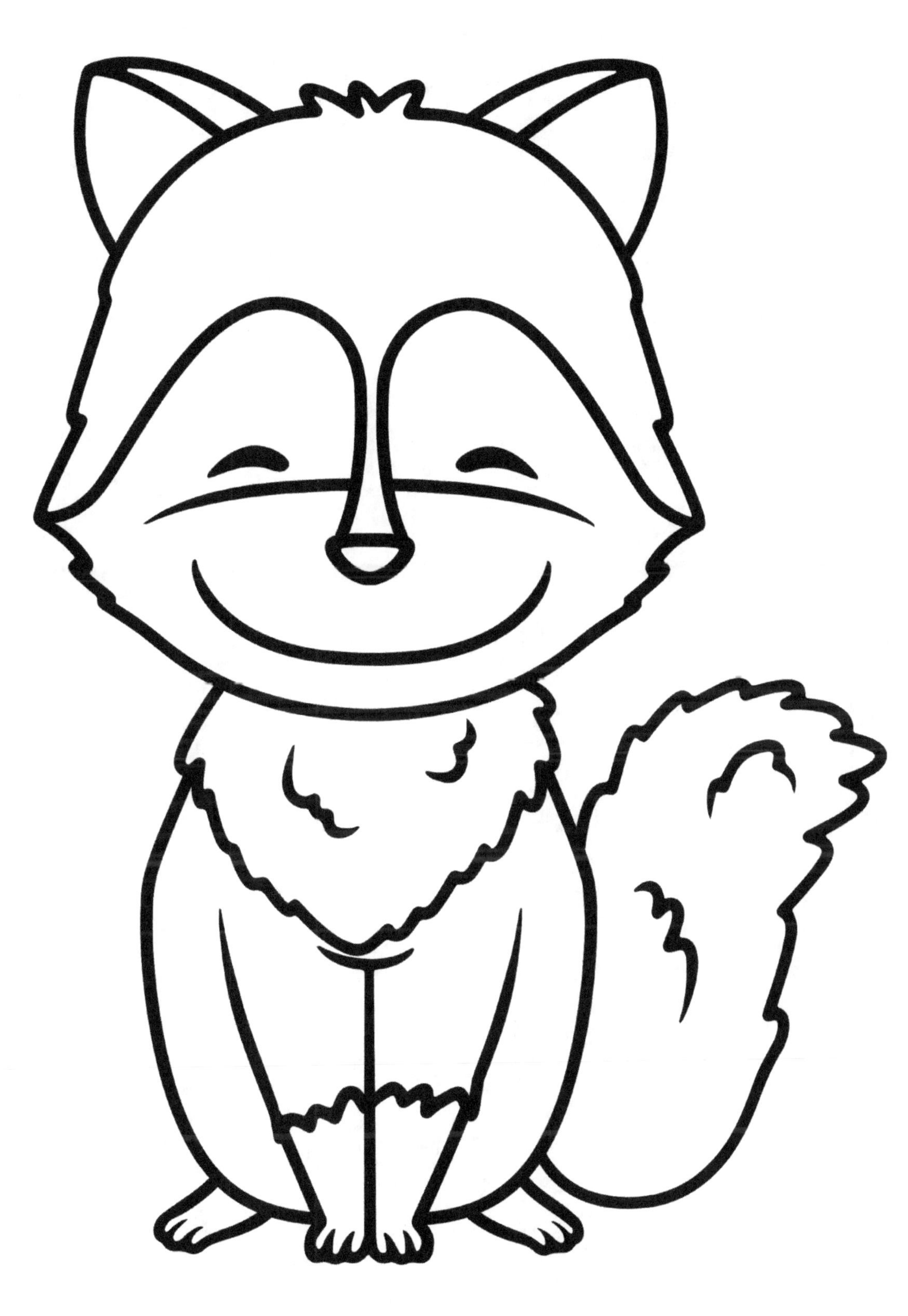

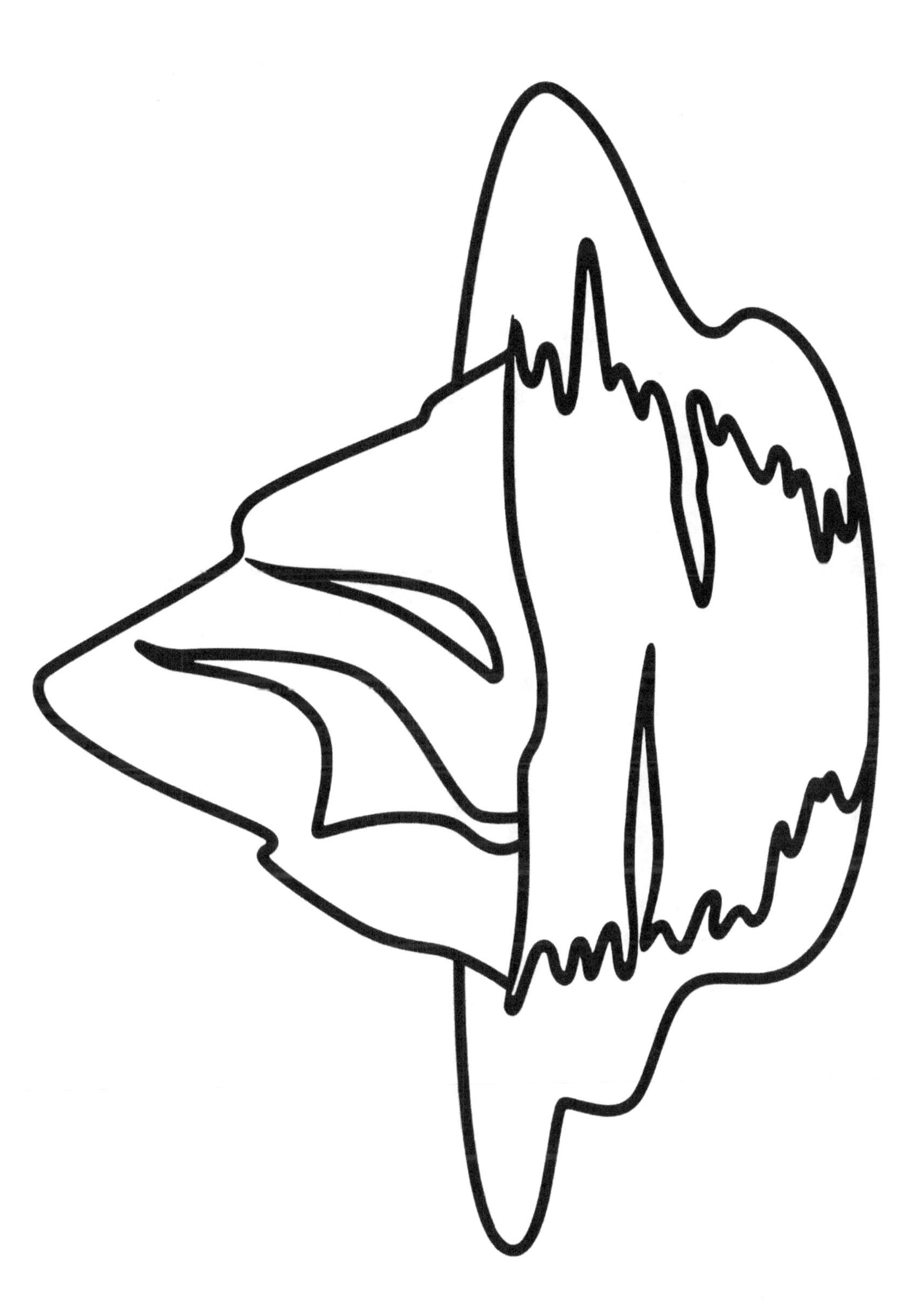

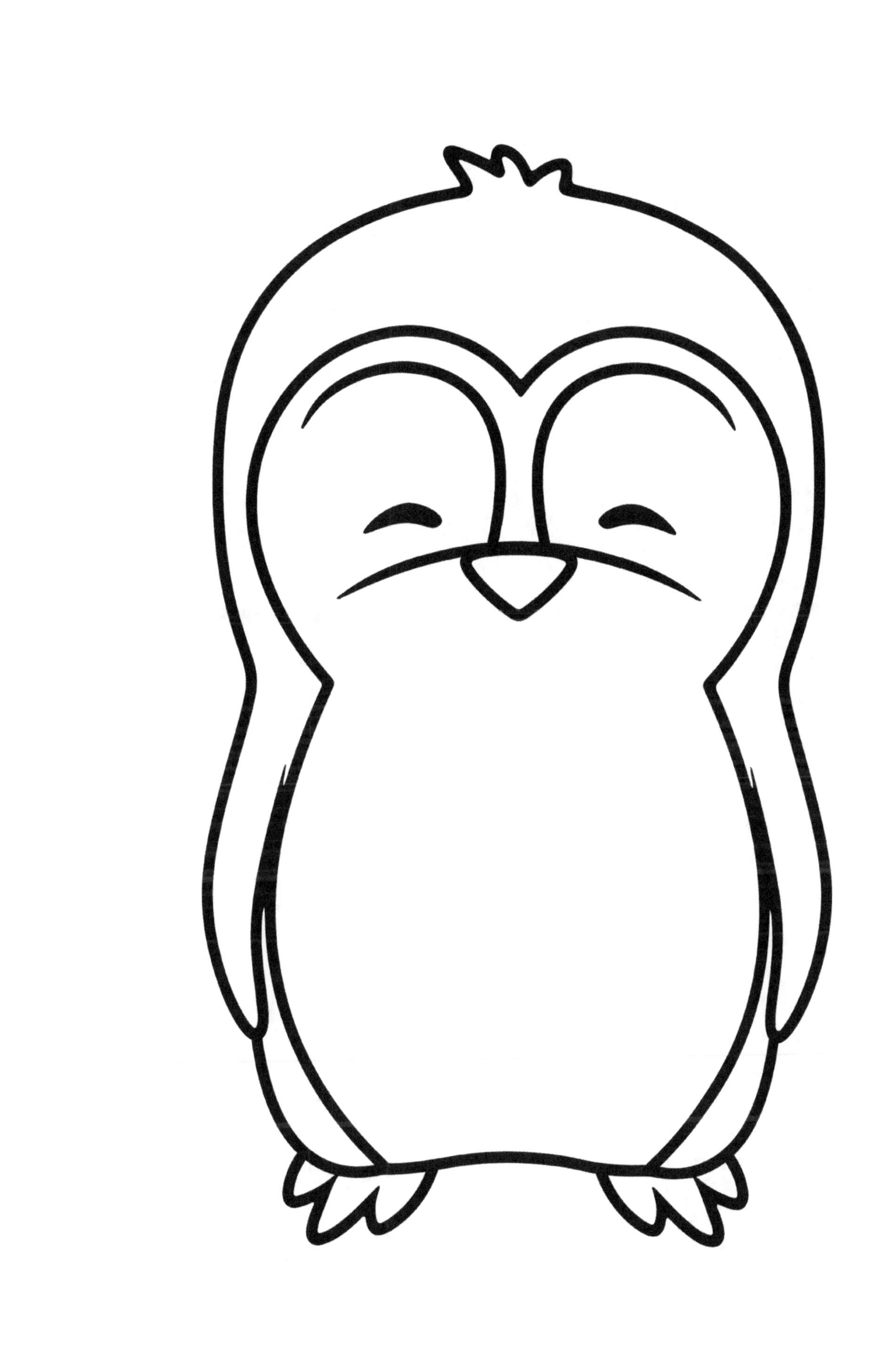

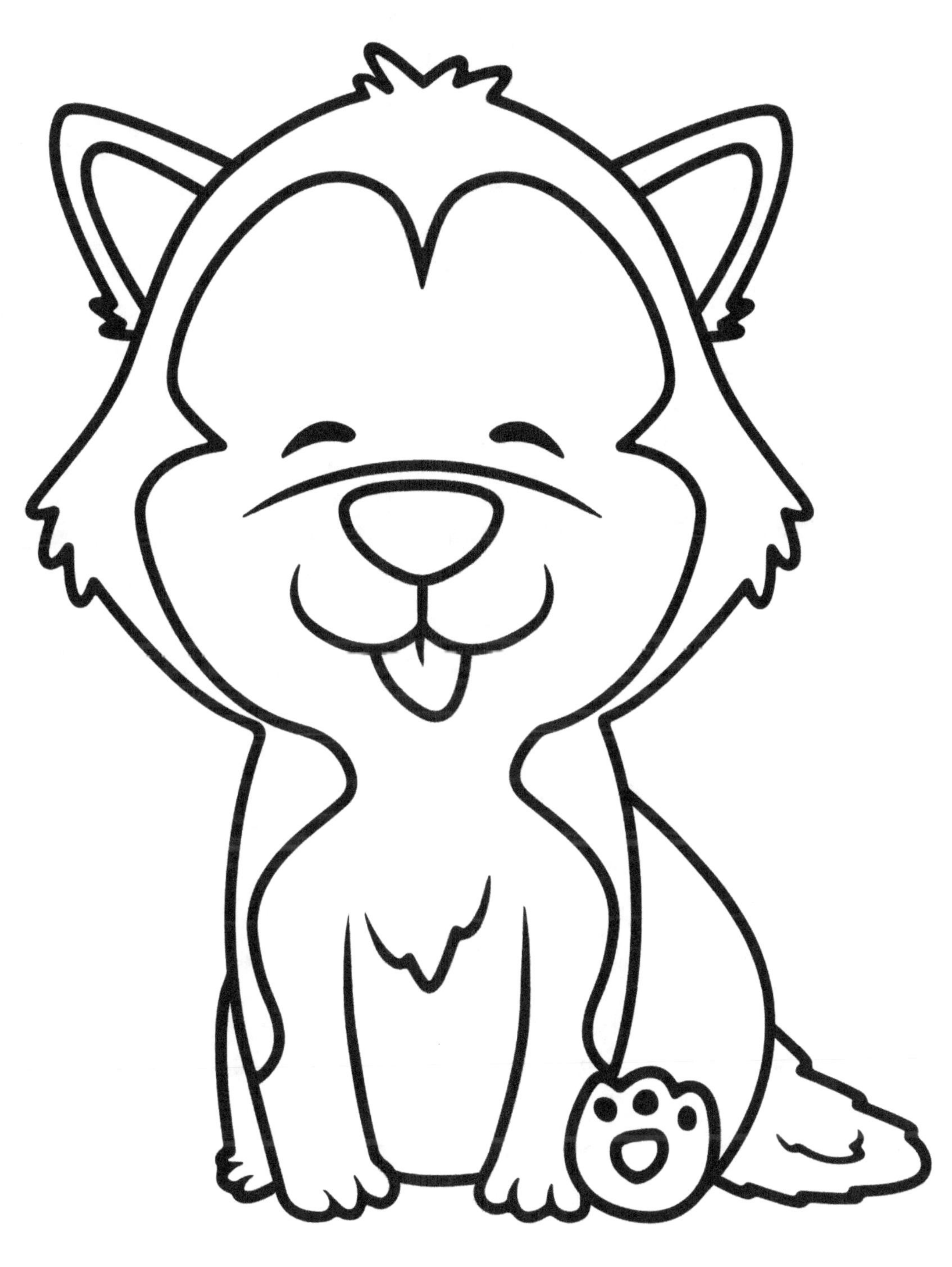

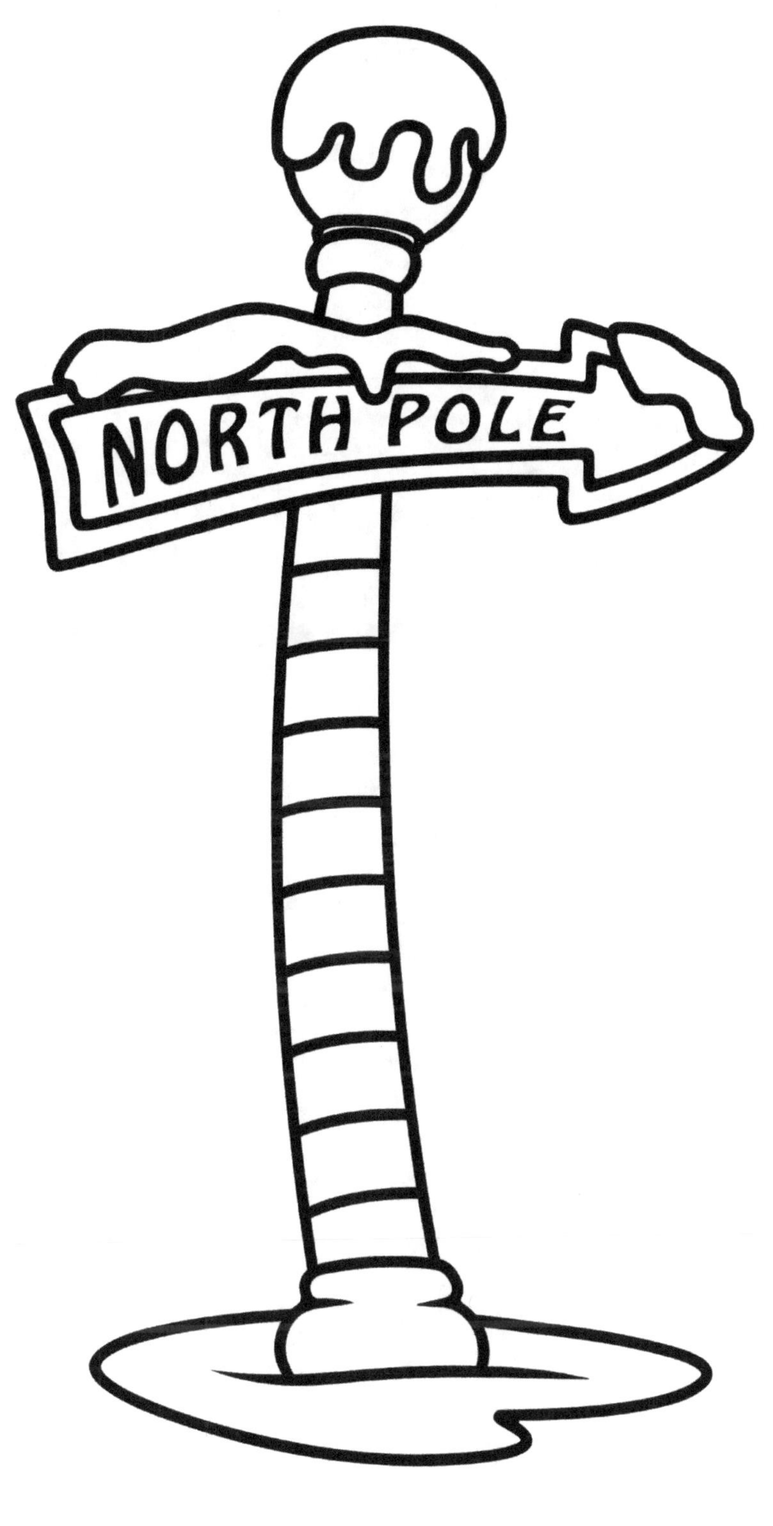
NORTH POLE

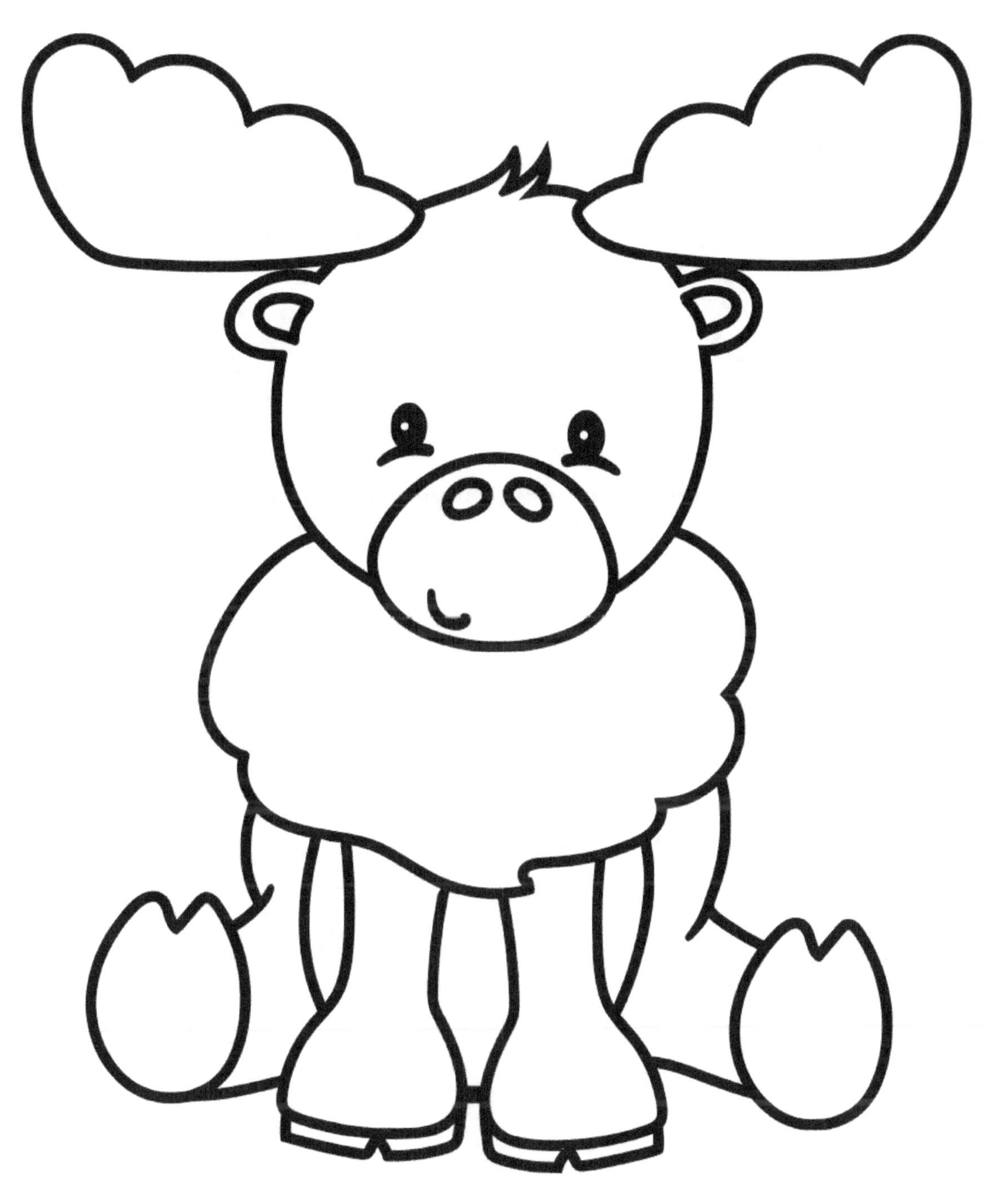

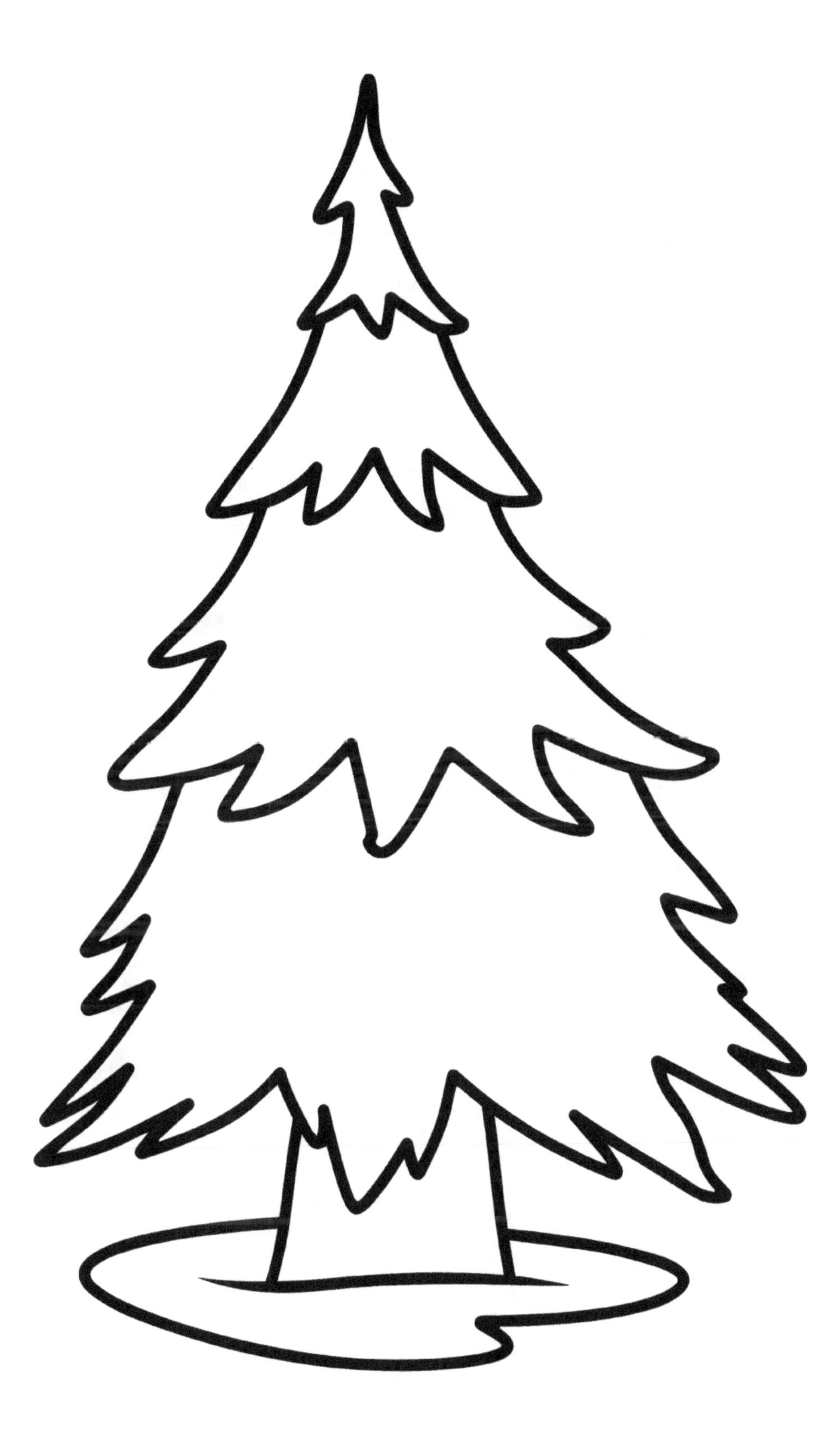

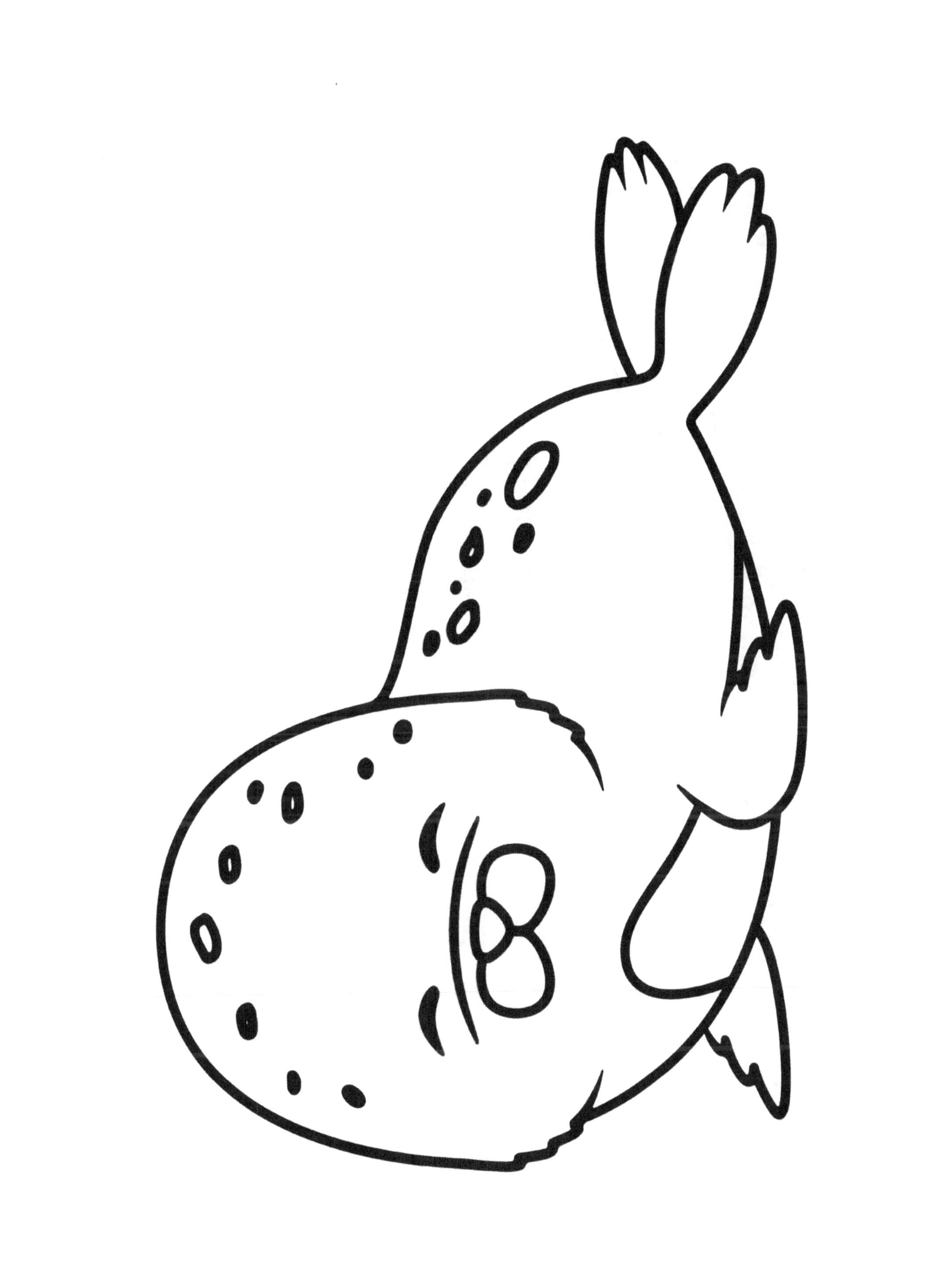

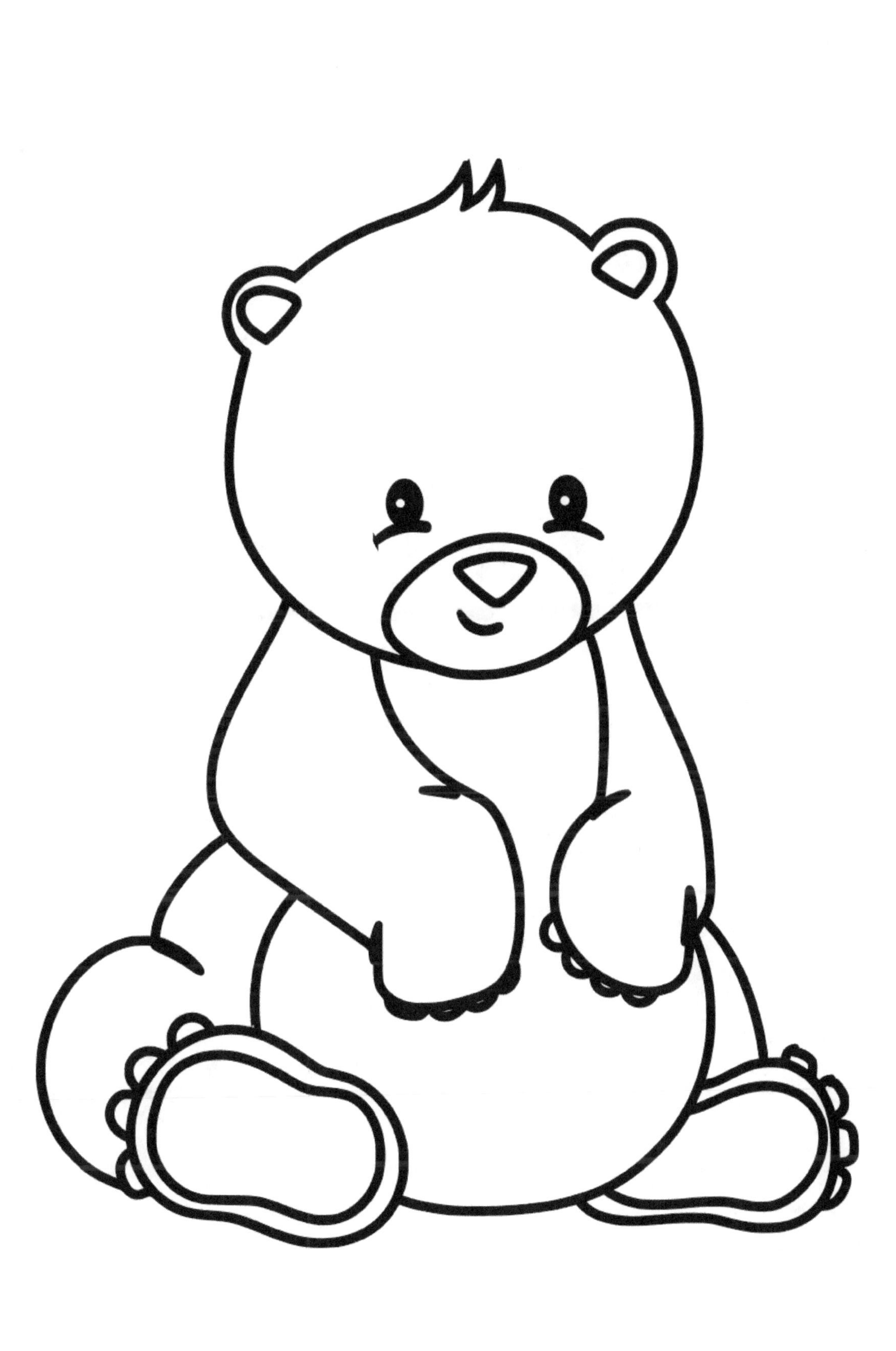

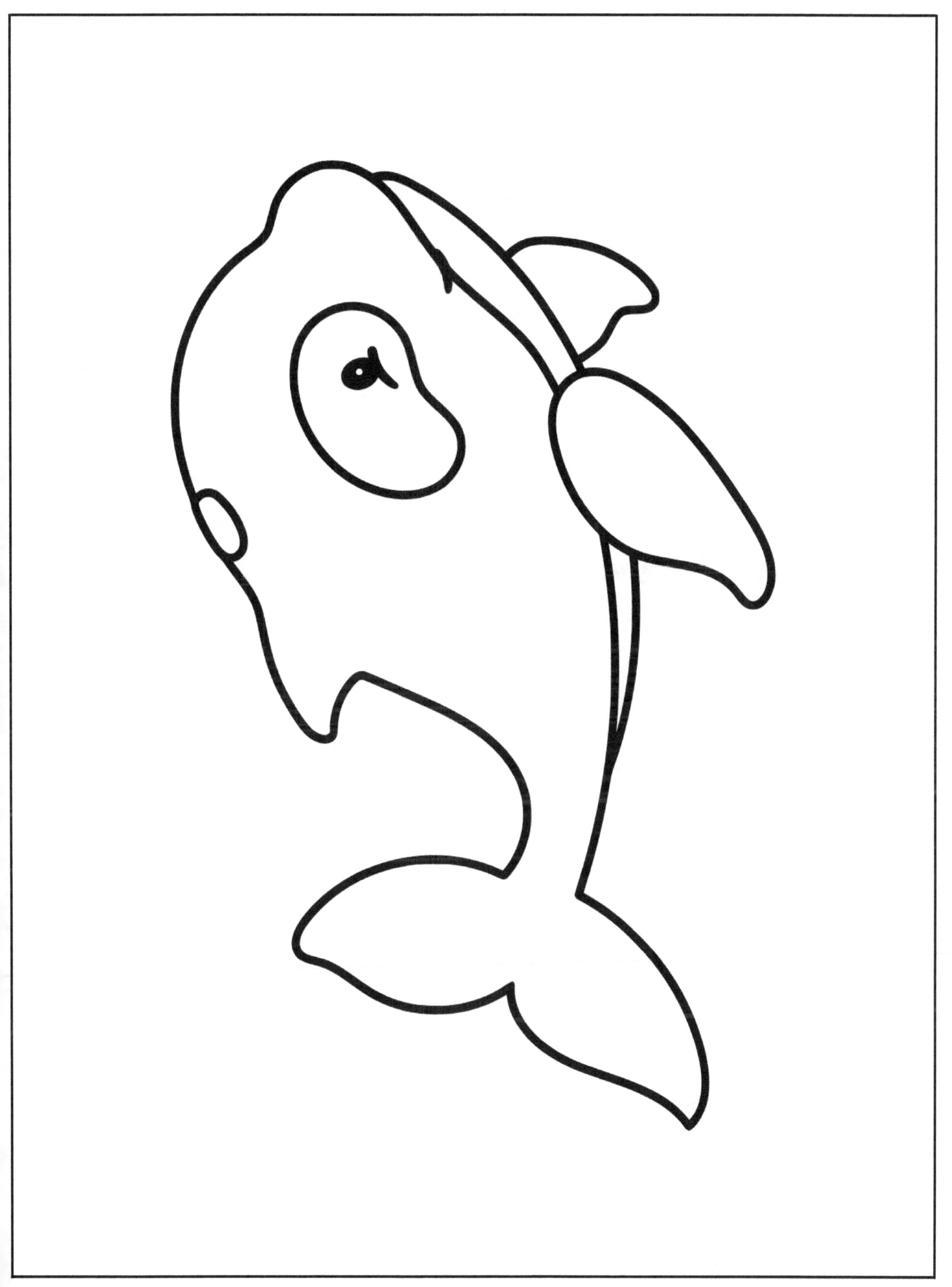

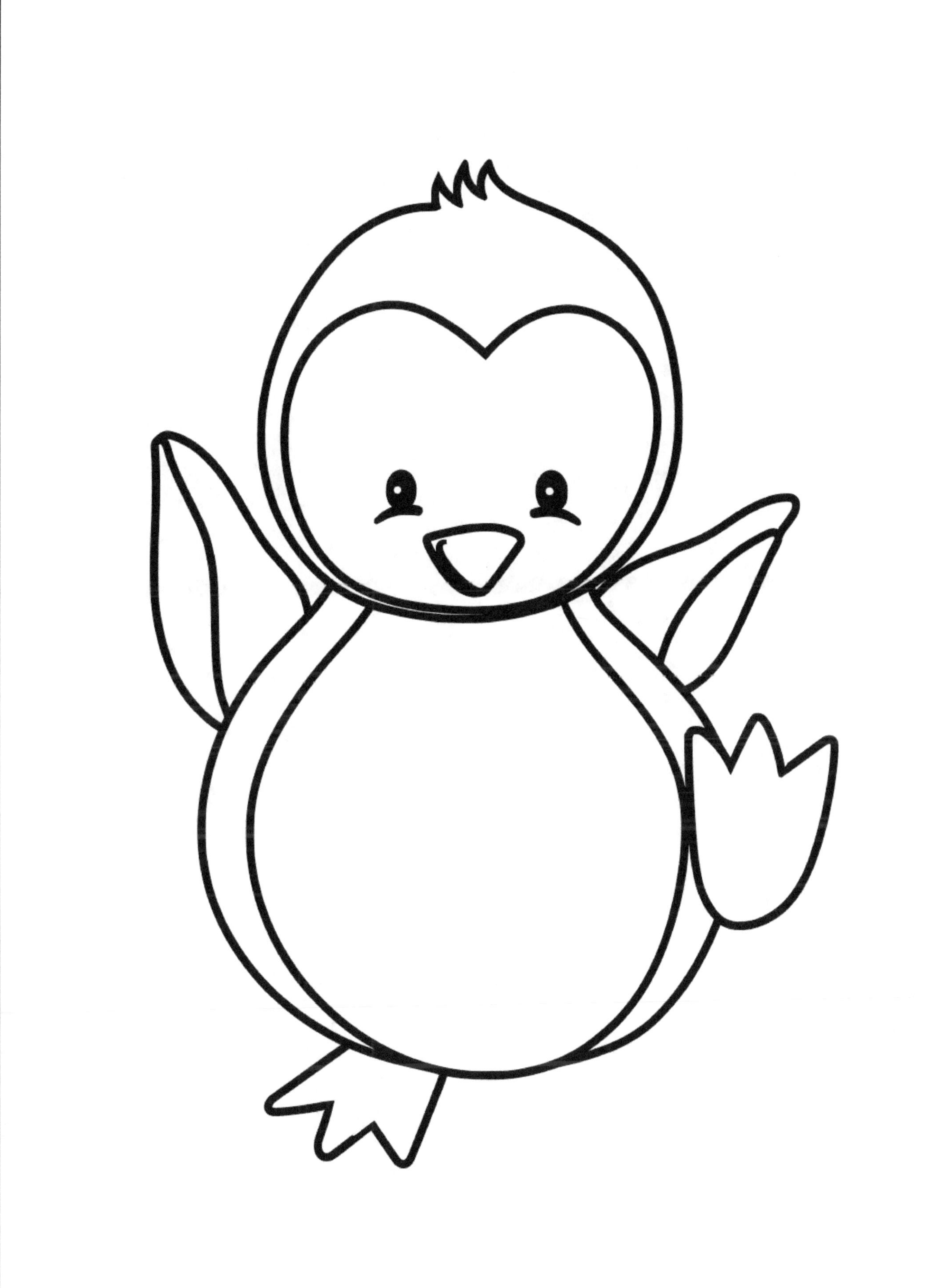

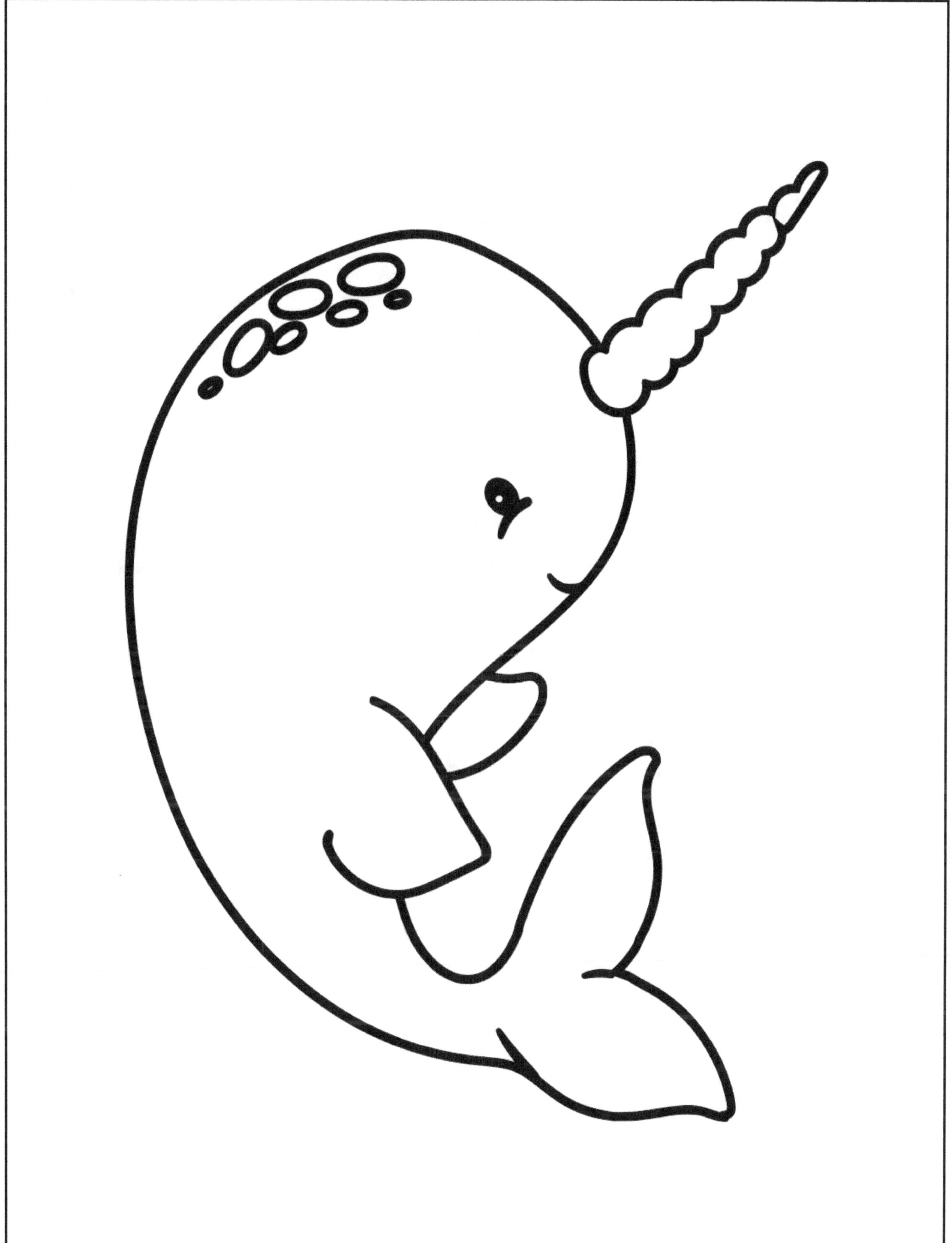

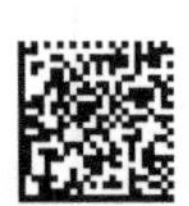